Poet aring 2

ster

Contents

OXFORD
UNIVERSITY PRESS

Parrot

Sometimes I sit with both eyes closed,
But all the same, I've heard:
They're saying, "He won't talk because
He is a *thinking* bird."

I'm olive-green and sulky, and
The family say, "Oh, yes,
He's silent, but he's *listening*,
He *thinks* more than he says!

"He ponders on the things he hears,
Preferring not to chatter."
– And this is true, but *why* it's true
Is quite another matter.

I'm working out some shocking things
In order to surprise them,
And when my thoughts are ready I'll
Certainly *not* disguise them!

I'll wait, and see, and choose a time
When everyone is present,
And clear my throat and raise my beak
And give a squawk and start to speak
And go on for about a week
And it will not be pleasant!

Alan Brownjohn

Chameleon

I can think sharply
and I can change:
my colours cover a considerable range.

I can be some mud by
an estuary,
I can be a patch on the bark of a tree.

I can be green grass
or a little thin stone
– or if I really want to be left alone,

I can be a shadow. …
What I am on your
multi-coloured bedspread, I am not quite sure.

Alan Brownjohn

Rat It Up

A poem for two or more voices

C'mon everybody
Slap some grease on those paws
Get some yellow on your teeth
And, uh, sharpen your claws

There's a whole lot of sausage
We're gonna swallow down
We're gonna jump out the sewers
And rock this town

Cos we're rattin' it up
Yes we're rattin' it up
Well we're rattin' it up
For a ratting good time tonight!

Ain't got no compass
You don't need no map
Just follow your snout
Hey, watch out for that trap!

You can take out a poodle
Beat up a cat
But if you can't lick a ferret
You ain't no kind of rat

Cos we're rattin' it up
Yes we're rattin' it up
Well we're rattin' it up
For a ratting good time tonight!

Now you can sneak in the henhouse
You can roll out the eggs
But if the farmer comes running
Bite his hairy legs

Check that cheese for poison
Before you eat
Or you'll wind up being served up
As ratburger meat

Cos we're rattin' it up
Yes we're rattin' it up
Well we're rattin' it up
For a ratting good time tonight!

This rat was born to rock
This rat was born to roll
I don't give a monkey's
'Bout your pest control

So push off pussy-cat
And push off pup
We're the Rocking Rodents
And we're ratting it up

Yeah we're rattin' it up
Yeah we're rattin' it up
Well we're rattin' it up
For a ratting good time tonight!

Adrian Mitchell

Creature

I am
the crazy
crater creature,
I creep across the
crater 's cracks
and cr u nch the
crimson crystals
that cringe in
crooked cul-de-sacs.
Once a crumbling spacecraft crashed—
an ancient cosmonaut crawled clear.
Across the crinkled crust I chased her
and chortling with churlish cheer
caught the granny
in a cranny
of the crater
and ate her

Dave Calder

Dodo

LITTLE BRAIN
So sLoW
FAT BODY
WINGS CAN'T FLY
HoHo!
SHORT LEGS
NONo.
WON'T GoGo.
NOW DEFUNCT
DODO

Jenny Morris

A Yak from the Hills of Iraq

A yak from the hills of Iraq
Met a yak he had known awhile
back.
   They went out to dine
   And talked of lang syne –
Yak-ety, yak-ety, yak.

Willard R. Espy

Spellbound

I have a spelling chequer
It came with my PC
It plainly marks four my revue
Miss takes I cannot sea.
I've run this poem threw it
I'm shore your pleased too no;
It's letter perfect in it's weigh
My chequer tolled me sew.

Norman Vandal

An Acrostic

A favourite literary devi
Ce is the one whe
Re the first letter
Of each line spell
S out the subject the poe
T wishes to write about.
I must admit, I
Can't see the point myself.

Roger McGough

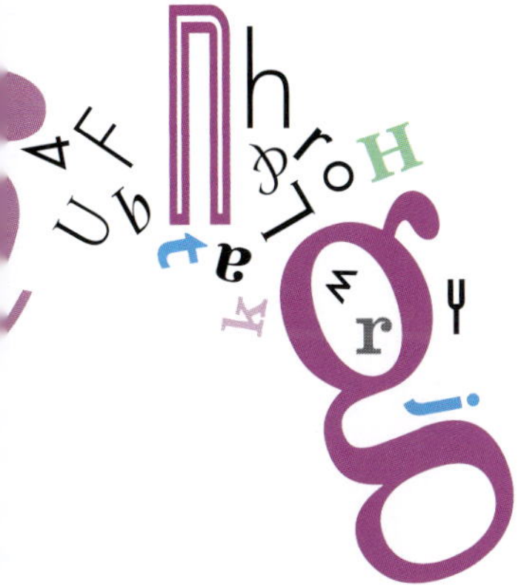

Jelly and Melons

When Jilly eats jelly,
Then Jilly is jolly.
But melons make Melanie
Most melancholy.

Colin West

Excuses, Excuses!

A poem for two voices

Late again, Blenkinsopp?
What's the excuse this time?
Not my fault, sir.
Whose fault is it then?
Grandma's, sir.
Grandma's? What did she do?
She died, sir.
Died?
She's seriously dead all right, sir.
That makes four grandmothers this term, Blenkinsopp
And all on P.E. days.
I know. It's very upsetting, sir.

How many grandmothers have you got, Blenkinsopp?
Grandmothers sir? None, sir.
You said you had four.
All dead, sir.
And what about yesterday, Blenkinsopp?
What about yesterday, sir?
You were absent yesterday.
That was the dentist, sir.
The dentist died?
No sir. My teeth, sir.
You missed the maths test, Blenkinsopp!
I'd been looking forward to it, sir.
Right, line up for P.E.
Can't, sir.
No such word as "can't", Blenkinsopp.
No kit, sir.
Where is it?
Home, sir.
What's it doing at home?
Not ironed, sir.
Couldn't you iron it?
Can't, sir.
Why not?
Bad hand, sir.
Who usually does it?
Grandma, sir.
Why couldn't she do it?
Dead, sir.

Gareth Owen

Trout

Hangs, a fat gun-barrel,
deep under arched bridges
or slips like butter down
the throat of the river.

From the depths smooth-skinned as plums
his muzzle gets bull's eye;
picks off grass-seed and moths
that vanish, torpedoed.

Where water unravels
over gravel-bed he
is fired from the shallows
white belly reporting

flat; darts like a tracer-
bullet back between stones
and is never burnt out.
A volley of cold blood

ramrodding the current.

Seamus Heaney

Fishing

I have waited with a long rod
And suddenly pulled a gold-and-greenish,
   lucent fish from below,
And had him fly like a halo round my head,
Lunging in the air on the line.

Unhooked his gorping, water-horny mouth,
And seen his horror-tilted eye,
His red-gold, water-precious, mirror-flat bright eye;
And felt him beat in my hand, with his mucous,
   leaping life-throb.

D. H. Lawrence

The Sea

They wash their hands in it.
The salt turns to soap
In their hands. Wearing it
At their wrists, they make bracelets
Of it; it runs in beads
On their jackets. A child's
Plaything? It has hard whips
That it cracks, and knuckles
To pummel you. It scrubs
And scours; it chews rocks
To sand; its embraces
Leave you without breath. Mostly
It is a stomach, where bones,
Wrecks, continents are digested.

R. S. Thomas

Break, Break, Break

Break, break, break,
   On thy cold gray stones, O Sea!
And I would that my tongue could utter
   The thoughts that arise in me.

O well for the fisherman's boy
   That he shouts with his sister at play!
O well for the sailor lad,
   That he sings in his boat on the bay!

And the stately ships go on
   To their haven under the hill;
But O for the touch of a vanish'd hand
   And the sound of a voice that is still.

Break, break, break
   At the foot of thy crags, O Sea!
But the tender grace of a day that is dead
   Will never come back to me.

Alfred, Lord Tennyson

The Song of the Whale

Heaving mountain in the sea,
Whale, I heard you
Grieving.

Great whale, crying for your life,
Crying for your kind, I knew
How we would use
Your dying:

Lipstick for our painted faces,
Polish for our shoes.

Tumbling mountain in the sea,
Whale, I heard you
Calling.

Bird-high notes, keening, soaring:
At their edge a tiny drum
Like a heartbeat.

We would make you
Dumb.

In the forest of the sea,
Whale, I heard you
Singing.

Singing to your kind.
We'll never let you be.
Instead of life we choose

Lipstick for our painted faces
Polish for our shoes.

Kit Wright

Miller's End

When we moved to Miller's End,
   Every afternoon at four
A thin shadow of a shade
   Quavered through the garden-door.

Dressed in black from top to toe
   And a veil about her head
To us all it seemed as though
   She came walking from the dead.

With a basket on her arm
Through the hedge-gap she would pass,
Never a mark that we could spy
On the flagstones or the grass.

When we told the garden-boy
How we saw the phantom glide,
With a grin his face was bright
As the pool he stood beside.

"That's no ghost-walk," Billy said,
"Nor a ghost you fear to stop –
Only old Miss Wickerby
On a short cut to the shop."

So next day we lay in wait,
Passed a civil time of day,
Said how pleased we were she came
Daily down our garden-way.

Suddenly her cheek it paled,
Turned, as quick, from ice to flame.
"Tell me," said Miss Wickerby.
"Who spoke of me, and my name?"

"Bill the garden-boy."
She sighed,
Said, "Of course, you could not know
How he drowned – that very pool –
A frozen winter – long ago."

Charles Causley

The Man He Killed

"Had he and I but met
By some old ancient inn,
We should have sat us down to wet
Right many a nipperkin!

"But ranged as infantry,
And staring face to face,
I shot at him as he at me,
And killed him in his place.

"I shot him dead because –
Because he was my foe,
Just so: my foe of course he was:
That's clear enough; although

"He thought he'd 'list, perhaps,
Off-hand like – just as I –
Was out of work – had sold his traps –
No other reason why.

"Yes; quaint and curious war is!
You shoot a fellow down
You'd treat if met where any bar is,
Or help to half-a-crown."

Thomas Hardy

"It Isn't Right to Fight"

You said, "It isn't right to fight."
But when we watched the news tonight,
You shook your fist and said
You wished the tyrant and his cronies dead.
When I asked why,
If it's not right to fight,
You gave a sigh.
You shook your head
And sadly said,
"Sometimes a cause is just
And, if there is no other way,
Perhaps, you must."

John Foster

Song of Hope

At that hour
when the sun
slinks off
behind hills
and night
– a panther –
crouches
ready to spring
upon our un-
suspecting city …

i want to sing
the coiled desires
of this land
the caged dreams
of forgotten men

i want to sing
of all that was
but no longer is
of all that
never was but
could have been

i want to sing
the obsidian
unspelled hopes
of our children
i want to sing
to remind us
never to despair
that every hour
every minute
somewhere on the face
of this earth
it is glorious morning.

Cecil Rajendra

Christmus a Come (Christmas is Coming)

De fee-fee dem come out big an bright,
An everywhey yuh go
Pickney a pick de fee-fee dem
An a blow dem loud yuh know.

De poinsettia leaf dem change from green
And turn as red as blood,
One turkey eena de fowl coop
A get fatten up fe food.

De sorrel red, it soon ready
Fe bwile up wid de wine,
An Papa sey de gungo peas
An yellow yam doing fine.

So we soon start fe have gungo soup
De orange dem a ripe,
An breeze start blow soh cold now
Mi haffe wear sweater go a stan-pipe.

Me sista a mek Gran-market frock
Mama soaking fruits fe bake
An Pape buy one crate a wine
An some rum fe soak de cake.

De ginger dem a blossom,
Me eat one tangerine today,
An only two week lef now
Before school gi holiday.

Everytime me turn on de radio
Me hear Chrismus carol a play,
So me know fe sure sey Chrismus a come,
Yes, bwoy, Chrismus pon de way.

Valerie Bloom

Still

Snow, finer than crushed glass,
Falls continuously,
Smothering road and roof
Until the day shivers
To a Christmas card still.

Buried, the earth's slowed pulse
Weathers this deep season.

Wes Magee

School Field in Winter

Hundreds of Wellington boots
Have hard-packed the snow until
The field glitters like a rink.

Snowmen stand rigid with cold.
Squeals of children skate across
An acre of Arctic ice.

Wes Magee

Christmas Landscape

Tonight the wind gnaws
With teeth of glass,
The jackdaw shivers
In caged branches of iron,
The stars have talons.

There is hunger in the mouth
Of vole and badger,
Silver agonies of breath
In the nostril of the fox.

Laurie Lee

Xmas

Not a twig stirs. The frost-bitten garden
Huddles under a heaped duvet of snow.
Pond, tree, sky and street are granite with cold.

In the house, electronic games warble:
Holly awaits the advent of balloons,
And the TV set glows tipsy with joy.

Wes Magee

Stopping by Woods on a Snowy Evening

Whose woods these are I think I know.
His house is in the village though;
He will not see me stopping here
To watch his woods fill up with snow.

My little horse must think it queer
To stop without a farmhouse near
Between the woods and frozen lake
The darkest evening of the year.

He gives his harness bells a shake
To ask if there is some mistake.
The only other sound's the sweep
Of easy wind and downy flake.

The woods are lovely, dark and deep,
But I have promises to keep,
And miles to go before I sleep,
And miles to go before I sleep.

Robert Frost

Change

The summer
still hangs
heavy and sweet
with sunlight
as it did last year.

The autumn
still comes
showering gold and crimson
as it did last year.

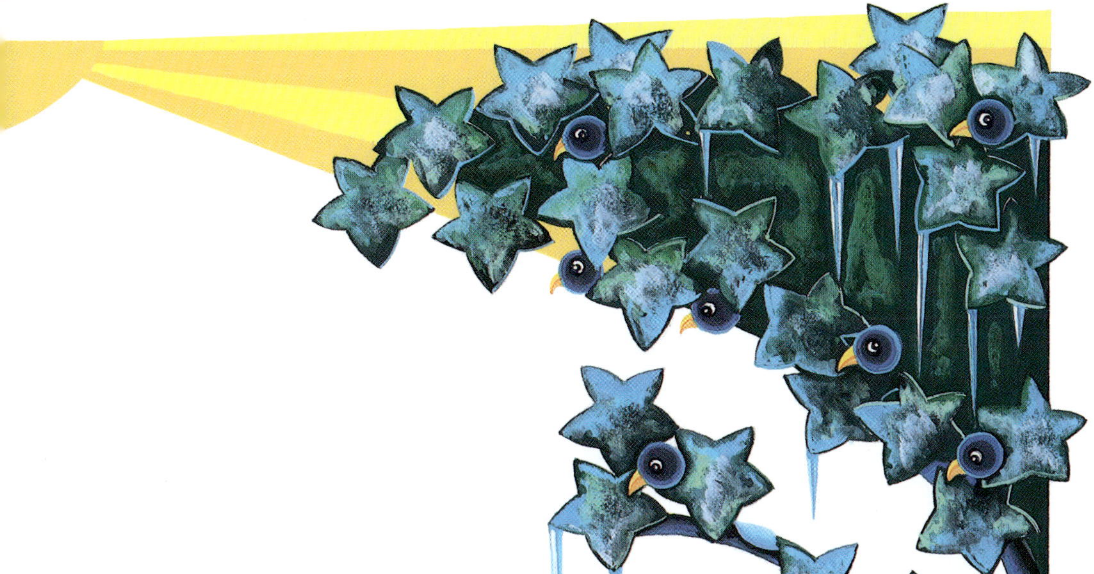

The winter
still stings
clean and cold and white
as it did last year.

The spring
still comes
like a whisper in the dark night.

It is only I
who have changed.

Charlotte Zolotow

OXFORD
UNIVERSITY PRESS
Great Clarendon Street, Oxford OX2 6DP

Oxford University Press is a department of the University of Oxford.
It furthers the University's objective of excellence in research, scholarship, and education by publishing worldwide in

Oxford New York
Athens Auckland Bangkok Bogotá Buenos Aires Calcutta
Cape Town Chennai Dar es Salaam Delhi Florence Hong Kong Istanbul
Karachi Kuala Lumpur Madrid Melbourne Mexico City Mumbai
Nairobi Paris São Paulo Singapore Taipei Tokyo Toronto Warsaw

and associated companies in Berlin Ibadan

First published 1999

British Library Cataloguing in publication Data
Data available

ISBN 0 19 834186 5

Also available as a Big Book
Poetry for Sharing 2 Big Book ISBN 0 19 834187 3

Printed in Hong Kong

Acknowledgements

The Editor and Publisher are grateful for permission to reprint the following copyright poems previously published by Oxford University Press:

Valerie Bloom for 'Christmus a Come' first published in John Foster (ed): *Another Third Poetry Book* (OUP) Copyright © Valerie Bloom 1987, by permission of the author; Alan Brownjohn for 'Parrot' and 'Chameleon' from *Brownjohn's Beasts*, by permission of the publishers, Macmillan Children's Books London; Dave Calder for 'Creature' first published in John Foster (ed): *Wordwhirls* (OUP) Copyright © Dave Calder 1998, by permission of the author; Charles Causley for 'Millers End' from *Figgie Hobbin*, by permission of David Higham Associates; Willard R Espy for 'A Yak from the Hills of Iraq', first published in John Foster (ed): *Crack Another Yolk* (OUP), Copyright © Willard R Espy 1996; John Foster for 'It Isn't Right to Fight' first published in *Standing on the Sidelines* (OUP), Copyright © John Foster 1995, by permission of the author; Robert Frost for 'Stopping by Woods on a Snowy Evening' from *The Poetry of Robert Frost* edited by R Connery Lathem (Jonathan Cape/Henry Holt), Copyright 1942, 1944, 1951, © 1962 by Robert Frost, © 1970 by Lesley Frost Ballantine, Copyright 1916, 1923, 1934, © 1969 by Henry Holt and Company, Inc, by permission of Henry Holt and Company, Inc and Random House UK Ltd on behalf of the Estate of Robert Frost; Seamus Heaney for 'Trout' from *Death of a Naturalist* (*New Selected Poems 1966-1987*) by permission of the publishers, Faber & Faber Ltd; also reprinted from Poems 1965-1975, Copyright © 1980 by Seamus Heaney, by permission of Farrar Straus & Giroux, Inc.; D H Lawrence for lines from 'Fish' from *The Complete Poems of D H Lawrence* edited by V de Sola Pinto & F W Roberts, Copyright © 1964 by Angelo Ravagli, and C M Weekley, Executors of the Estate of Frieda Lawrence Ravagli, by permission of Laurence Pollinger Limited, the Estate of Frieda Lawrence Ravagli, and Viking Penguin, a division of Penguin Putnam Inc.; Laurie Lee for 'Christmas Landscape' from *Selected Poems* (Penguin), by permission of the Peters Fraser & Dunlop Group Ltd.; Roger McGough for 'An Acrostic' from *Nailing the Shadow* (Viking Kestrel), by permission of the Peters Fraser & Dunlop Group Ltd.; Wes Magee for 'Still', 'Xmas' and 'School Field in Winter' first published in John Foster (ed): *A Fifth Poetry Book* (OUP), Copyright © Wes Magee 1985, all by permission of the author; Adrian Mitchell for 'Rat It Up' © Adrian Mitchell, from *Balloon Lagoon and the Magic Islands of Poetry* (Orchard Books, 1997) by permission of the Peters Fraser and Dunlop Group Limited on behalf of Adrian Mitchell. Educational Health Warning! Adrian Mitchell asks that none of his poems are used in comnection with any examinations whatsoever; Jenny Morris for 'Dodo' first published in John Foster (ed): *Crack Another Yolk* (OUP), Copyright © Jenny Morris 1996, by permission of the author; Gareth Owen for 'Excuses, Excuses!' originally called 'Conversation Piece' from *Salford Road and Other Poems* (Young Lions, 1988), Copyright © Gareth Owen 1988, by permission of the author c/o Rogers Coleridge & White, 20 Powis Mews, London W11 1NJ; R S Thomas for 'The Sea' from *The Way of It* (Ceolfrith Press, 1977) Copyright © R S Thomas 1977, by permission of the author; Colin West for 'Jelly and Melons' from *Not to be Taken Seriously* (Hutchinson), Copyright © Colin West, by permission of the author; Kit Wright for 'Song of the Whale' from *Hot Dog and Other Poems* (Kestrel 1981), Copyright © Kit Wright 1981, by permission of Penguin Books Ltd; Charlotte Zolotow for 'Change' from *River Winding*, Copyright © 1970 by Charlotte Zolotow, reprinted by permission of Scott Treimel New York for the author.

Despite efforts to obtain permission from all copyright holders before publication, this has not been possible in a few cases. If notified, the publisher will be pleased to rectify any errors or omissions at the earliest opportunity.

The illustrations are by:

Allan Curless pp 2–3;
Paul Dowling pp 10–11;
Tudor Humphries pp 20–21, 26–27;
Robert Kettell pp 14–15, 18;
Peter Lubach pp 4–5;
Valerie McBride pp 30–31;
Sheila Moxley pp 24–25;
Jane Strother pp 28–29;
Rachel Ross pp 12–13, 17;
Rosemary Woods p 22–23